Sex Augury

Sex Augury

poems

C. BAIN

🐔 Red Hen Press | *Pasadena, CA*

Book design by Mark E. Cull

Library of Congress Cataloging-in-Publication Data

Names: Bain, C. (Artist), author.
Title: Sex augury: poems / C. Bain.
Description: Pasadena, CA: Red Hen Press, [2023]
Identifiers: LCCN 2023022175 (print) | LCCN 2023022176 (ebook) | ISBN
  9781636281322 (paperback) | ISBN 9781636281339 (ebook)
Subjects: LCGFT: Poetry.
Classification: LCC PS3602.A5586 S49 2023 (print) | LCC PS3602.A5586
  (ebook) | DDC 811/.6—dc23/eng/20230512
LC record available at https://lccn.loc.gov/2023022175
LC ebook record available at https://lccn.loc.gov/2023022176

Publication of this book has been made possible in part through the generous financial
support of Ann Beman.

The National Endowment for the Arts, the Los Angeles County Arts Commission, the Ahmanson
Foundation, the Dwight Stuart Youth Fund, the Max Factor Family Foundation, the Pasadena
Tournament of Roses Foundation, the Pasadena Arts & Culture Commission and the City of
Pasadena Cultural Affairs Division, the City of Los Angeles Department of Cultural Affairs,
the Audrey & Sydney Irmas Charitable Foundation, the Meta & George Rosenberg Foundation,
the Albert and Elaine Borchard Foundation, the Adams Family Foundation, Amazon Literary
Partnership, the Sam Francis Foundation, and the Mara W. Breech Foundation partially support
Red Hen Press.

First Edition
Published by Red Hen Press
www.redhen.org

this is for Jordan

CONTENTS

Sex Augury

You Can Perform Divination in Any Material

even like this   shoving the mirror
between my legs   it's turned weapon-multiple
mechanical   saw tipped arms flailing
tearing its halo   of too-fine skin
the new exoskeleton   builds itself
                    under the old

then breaks away
the inside becomes
        the surface   the surface, something
       dead you leave behind

It had taken over   without me
knowing it. Phone calls   to the president.
Remotely piloting   fighter jets.
It wasn't ever again   what they had warned
something to   pity and repair.

This girl is asking me if it feels better now
transition. If it's helped. If i am comfortable.
Bombs shucking themselves out their metal casings
to hurl shrapnel and fire into running bodies

i tell the girl   comfort is relative
some things can never be corrected
the buckling wall   between myself and myself
succumbs to flame.

It grows more legs   arachnoid scrambling away
i'm hissing at my crotch
Stop it.   *We are a person*
don't make me   *cauterize don't make*
me chemically   *castrate*
don't make me   *say it again*

in exorcism the demon pleads
then threatens   then hurls
the possessed   body against the wall   a weapon
against itself   against its savior.
Not everyone survives.

Maybe the evil is what held it all together.
Even if the patient lives
        they excrete little flames
                wisps of sulfur
the whole rest of their abandoned normal life.

Baby Mars

in a red lip. Honey Mars squeaks
quakes on the trigger. Tired.
There are places we can't come together
and in those places? Mars.
Rustochre icecapped queen

spiderfrost glittering.   O Mars   you
sent him to us   useless king
decay   dogtag stuffed in the toothgap

someone has to clean us up
keep us honest about what we need
that's Mars
who keeps the map
of futile crimes

Mars outlines you in chalk right where you stand
it's a good spot to die isn't it
how about where you are right now
            now   now   now
                                                            and now
afterward? *Whatever you want* Mars says.
A big white Daddy God and harps? wings? sure. shit.

                                        Mars says
conquest is the only art.
she says if you wanted another bitch
you should have never come to Mars

or come before when there was water
microbes, possibility, not now Honey
you're late. Inside yourself

fingers at war with the hands.
Hip at war with the joint of its socket.

You keep remembering Mars when you reach for joy
whose fault is that?
The fine sensations break down and then you need a slap

a cut line of powder
the tip of Mars's red tit.
Pleasure escapes and what is left? Only Mars.
Who wants to know
why you hate what you need.
to lose control.

you pay someone to have your dreams,
you pay to have the bodies taken out
walls scrubbed down
Mars runs her ice fingers through your hair.
Plastic cherry perfume
cough syrup cleaning fluid.
no battleaxes bonesaws that's the stuff
of personal vendetta. Mars is clean
and far away.

She elevates the data stream into
cash and cash into a relationship.
At some point, change your clothes, Mars says.
At some point, wash off the blood.

at some point the glass shatters
and the fine rain of clear stones
gives birth to a new shape
of you, if you survive

your own new craters
where Mars has kissed you.
This used to be water too.

Letter to Her Rapist

funny, to address you
as though you're singular.
As though what i need to say
can be said.   This   you also authored
          skinless god
anti-ink flying up from the paper
sound shoved back
through my throat until the glut of noise
splits me open

You know she left me?
Her bright bright heart.
The soft of her mouth
nearly forgotten alongside
the force of her mouth.
She leaves me. She never
leaves you. You've probably
forgotten it. A farmhouse.
Child you had because
you had the mother.
North of here. Cold at night.
She leaves me. She never leaves you.
She brings you with her
          everywhere.

(lies) (or, you could call it a lie)

Myths are not real. Race is a myth. Joan of Arc was killed not for hearing voices but for wearing men's clothes. Myths are not real but you can die of them. Monogamy. Absolute orientations. That you touch the wrong body and suddenly, you have lost yourself, your human mooring. The harp playing in the background. A thousand temperate floods. Myths are not real. Her bloodied hand. Her bloodied romper. The blank space inside my throat. i became microscopic, inhabiting frost mountains of her hair. Ice magic, her voice made of sugar and child promises, myths are not real. She held my hand on the subway. The men asking for money were all black. By design. Although i was told that it happens by coincidence. i was told it happens through evolution. i was told it is rude to notice it at all. The horizon beneath the airplane stretching. No one really wants this. A catalog of the body. Myths are not real. A dead animal recycled into nourishment. Cancer from plastics. Cancer from exhaust fumes. Exhaustion. That love will save you. i was told that it was nothing specific. Politics, too. Presidents, too. My parents. Flying into the dark, the entrails of your prey pouring out of your mouth. Please. Please, you were able to love me, that was love.

Metamorphosis (J train out of Kosciuszko)

there's a little girl on the train
with tight cornrows throwing herself
around the plastic seats
yelling while her parents stare
into space. She sees my hands

says *That man's*
wearing nail polish! That's so inappropriate!
Launches into the story of when grandma
took her to KFC but they couldn't eat
there because the cashier was a man

like that (Gay? Or faggot? i am
pretending to listen to music)
we elected someone and now my
body isn't safe the way this girl's
never was.

i go to 12 step meetings and cry
about it and men who lived
through AIDS without treatment
sit next to me saying *Back then a gay guy was like a*
$20 hooker you could kill them and
nothing would happen. A white man

shoots a 15 year old to
death for jostling him in a store then makes
his way home for dinner. (Suburbia. Ham-
burgers. god. A dog
who tears my liver out each night
and eats it. A dog

licking peanut butter off of
where ever you put it. The
one girl in middle school
less popular than me
was the one who
fucked dogs.
We grew up.
We are American adults.)

i am watching the eyes of my people
occluded and baking in
their own grease. Earth
splitting into white loam
then blood then harvest
skulls cracking on the
pavement and no wasps to plunder that
overrun sugar. Most of the time the most
important thing to me is still
that i'm alone. My hand opening
like a cunt. i meant that the
other way around.

Pornography in Wartime

Some new photographs are released
the hearty pink American
grinning through a coating of dust

his fist lifting the light head
of his thin civilian kill   severed
no accident
the compulsion to document

then click   click   new browser window
    i'm in
my bedroom   other bodies
move across the box of light
the famous poem
the girl   the swan's speculum beak
remember his hands winglike moving
through my face and the air around my face
when there were gods they would have stopped us
feathers battering my eyes
like snow or migraine
       (the first time i fainted it all
          went white)

men look at each other
across the woman's back
like acquaintances in a supermarket aisle
who do not know each other
well enough to say
         hello.

shoved whole through the eyesocket
white bulls in strange fields   swans bellowing

underneath this window the soldier is still open
goofy smile under the cartoonish bulge
of olive helmet another man walks into the frame
as though he has just arrived
erection wobbling
like a buoy on the surface of a lake

eventually it happens
my body's thousand swarming parts
flipped over
hard-shelled insects
with their legs twitching in air

fire comes from an invisible
machine in the sky
a satellite tracks acceptable civilian loss
the twitching wet orbs of my eyes
we come home and home is burning
if there were gods would they have stopped us?
or would they have taken pictures

what i've done during war i have done all my life
my skin   a screen
my skin an   eye
my skin dominion that keeps
me separate from the truth

i have never not been
in a nation at war

the position we find ourselves in
is always impossible   we are
half our fathers but men will not
admit to making us   so i walk
around in my half-man face   the
world horrified for me   so i wait
lycanthropic   for the moon to push
my blood out a furred mouth
everyone knows   i'm a monster
no one expects anything else

Venus

wants to hurt me forever. pink tongue tip in his mustache
a cigarette brushing my nipple
Does that hurt? he wants to know, laughing.
i can't believe i pay for this.

The glowing tip   smoke   small hairs
on my tit burning. Venus is known for brilliance. Heaven's point
pushing even into daylight.
How are you doing that? i'm drooling
a rag over my eyes.
How can you be both
the morning and the evening star

In reality Venus is larger
than Earth   oceans   clouds
everything made of acid.
it can't be lived in
You want me to
kiss it?! he says
dissolving in giggles

Venus rising on a bed of foam and inside
the clamshell this man who is a girl
who is a god who knows
and will not stop knowing me
houses fall into the acid ocean
tectonic   my name erased

Venus inside me
hourless king   cutting labryrinths into living rock
a man drawing maps

sewn into his sulfuric cloud
instead of one "set" of genitals he has
something like a toolbelt
drifting in the breeze
a tutu of naked mole rats
he shakes his ass

Love is the same god as ever
but nothing else
is made of what it used to be
                    formica
            particleboard spitting little slivers
into my tongue

Venus laughs. Love loves this.
Loves our dumb shit—how we can't
tell it apart   diamond or zircon
the inflatable vs. the real thing
every tool of love
is a weapon too

Love comes and she's a man
a cloud of acid, wolf-tongued
she comes and he is a man
with the reek of a thousand other bodies
nesting microbial in his pubes
which i know because my face is down there
i would like to have some pride, to be repulsed.
but no. Ravenous.

you want me to kiss it? to make it
better with my magic? his tongue
is in my mouth then a cloud

of acid is in my mouth then
the shining thing i thought
was love inside of me is a star
no is a planet no
is an orb
of acid bigger
than the world
and 27 million
miles away

Underworld

for MB, for Adam

        i'm in a hive of men
my back to the black painted wall
of the basement which seems
also to sweat   2 a.m.   i'm thinking

of Pasiphae who birthed the minotaur   No sun
here   light the color of blood
a beam struggling through an eyelid

Pasiphae   witch queen   oracular   brilliant
cursed with desire

crowd so thick it's hard even to move
i'm not disguised except
that i am here   so i must be a man

Pasiphae hid inside a sculpture
of a cow
because that's how badly she needed
the bull to fuck her.   lust was a punishment
a humiliation

what you love disfigures you
until you look like it   a boy   a mouth

ıllı

The men like dolphins climbing into the men like waves.
The room   a cow   a Trojan   a disguise
i'm struggling to part the velvet flood
for someone to unlock the mask

a bull three, five times
the dimensions of a man
hooves striking the earth.
sunlight gleaming
the slabs of muscle on the animal's back.

there must be
a moment when the bull knows
what it's doing

inside the sculpture
he's hooked into
a small wet howl

᭼

Pasiphae
Like you this is what i do
because no one loves me. Like you
i've learned to adore it.

᭼

when he found i could do that
pressed home and savage
not needing to be told
that loving me's a violence
not needing to be
shown
      the seafloor
          water pulling back

he finds i am a desert
                    serve
                            deserve
chamber behind the shutter of my throat
where i can keep a man instead of food or air
he smiles at me and i know how i look

From inside the disguise
still   and this is fatal
you wanted him to see your face
to know that it was you

                    ⑾

His sweat salt in his beard
tongue in my mouth
cock in its metal ring chemically hard

Can an animal even want you
can you call that *wanting* in the human sense

The ruff of hair against my face
filth where some other body
had just been wrapped around him

the bull at its cleanest
reeks of its own grassy shit
a red silk thread
cast through your nostrils
tugging your bowels
your cunt pulling itself
inside out to get to him

the party   the basement   hive of back rooms
the back of my body   my measure   i become
what i can accommodate

⫯⫯⫯

You say *woman*   woman
but my horns still grow
in the blood puddle inside of you
your dark inner mirror

is it power or only anatomy

This is how you bore me
mother
        This is what you made when
you wanted to know
what the monster would look like
if it came from your body.

they made a pill that keeps you from catching it

it's blue   what's stamped in its side
is *gilead* in capital letters
this is how they will know
where we are
          medication as surveillance
a puff of smoke and a man appears
i'm being paranoid
          he's not my man
he never died   no lesion ulcerated fungal
these are not allowed inside
but they curse the brain

the blood grows septic
i take a pill and nothing happens.
a virus blooms pink on every one of my lips and i live
and live   a puff of blue smoke
and a man says he can heal you
with a laying on of hands
the pharmacology is unclear to me
skin of his palms a thin red graft peeling
away   key clanking useless in the lock
of my cells   no pill for the fact
that i'm still who i am

exposure coming from inside
you take a pill and dicks sprout from the walls
silently weeping   a pill
and your terror's teeth fall out
it latches its soft bloody gums on your arm a pill
you're a ghost walking through latex walls

a pill and they come
back to you hospital gowns surged
across the threshold blinking
  why are we here they ask
why are you making us do this
dancing through the halls of your arteries
under the blinding chandelier

Campaign Advisement

In the infinite distance between revolution and governance
my dick begins a campaign for president. Phantasmagoric
filled with an uneasy magnetism.
You're pointing out that my dick is not literal, not concrete
enough in relation to the failures of nation-building
we can inarguably witness. But i say, what is my dick
if not aligned like a tracery over the architecture
of violence we have naturalized, accepted.
What is my dick if not a bridge built to commemorate a battle
fluted corinthian column slapped on the front of a brick colonial
Jackson, Rumsfeld, call him handsome, call him
philosopher-warrior, shadow king
say *No* to him and he finds a way to say you're being vague,
finds a way to say it into your mouth
until a soft assent echoes back, buckshot embedded
in your hunting buddy's face, that's my dick.
A founding father, fancy prose style, emerging variant,
ropes and ropes of hemp   cotton
      tobacco   data   the better
to ennoose you, the better to survive
your weight. My dick, frustrated
by waiting for openings drags itself to blood
against the granite pediments
refuses the containment of time
refuses negotiations that might lead
to its victory, refuses the techno-karmic advances
that would allow it to physically exist
so it's begun, of course, attacking me
scratching my skin inside, like the exorcist. i am tired
of explaining to you the unseen world water spooling upward
the ceiling a pool of trapped ghosts. You are tempted to use
fire but the fire will kill you too. Try to use flesh as a remedy

but whoops it's still your flesh the densest curse
of all, clasping my legs
around the obelisk, screaming

Don't take it away from me! That's my dick!

"*She's gone crazy, captain!*"

"*Well, lash her to the mast.
          A shame it isn't safe to burn a witch at sea.*"

What Saves a Boy in My Position is to Have Brothers

and i have no brothers. The zodiac unspools
a single shit-licking star
to signal me

no other soul under the celestial wheel
saddled with this. For no one i learn
and invent language
for no one i record my
history and when i go back in time
to see others like me i know we're alike only in that
we both are fully alien
alien from each other
too, the girl won't kiss me,
crying like an actress because she knows
we belong together, offworlders
and she's only hot for sons of earth.

What saves a boy in my position
is the cyanide capsule
hidden in the signet ring
or it's meant to, but they took it
my bootlaces too
every fatal ornament

What saves a boy
in my position carbon steel outer walls
collecting the unendurable heat
faulty organisms glassed-in, networked
scanned for virtue, redeemable habits
what saves—i wish they'd tell me.
i've never seen the evaluators
and suspect they don't exist
only once in every several months

i see some other boy like me
released, numb, stunned
wandering the corridor
massaging his own bruised wrists.

conception was his protest
not burst from the forehead   No i know
what part of his anatomy i rolled out of
my entered mother trying to soften it
stitch wings onto my back in the amniostasis
but she only made me a liar
wrapped me in flesh
that could not finally contain
who i had been before
who i would be again
a man outside   weeping
cursing the world for some debt
i was not actually owed

. . . and her severed head said to Perseus

⫴

The day i saw your ship
flyspeck on the horizon,
fear stormed in your heart
as you recognized
the stones that had been men.

i know you remember.
Try to brush it from your eyes
like a bad dream.
Telling Andromeda how you fought for her
whispering into the apricot nectar
of her hair, how brave you had been.

The sea was hammer dented steel—
you pulled yourself ashore.
The shield, one of the holy gifts
given you to conquer me
reflecting you back.

Shuffled toward me like a crab
sword stuck out behind you.
You looked ridiculous.
i had to do it myself
eyelashes crashing together like iron filings
i sunk my scaly neck into the blade.
The hissing protest in my head finally stilled.

i could see your reflection,
light pouring like blood out your face.
Dark, fallible flesh that you hide and flatter.
So close, i could smell

the inside of your mouth like wet silk.
Sick with fear,
sweat beading your wide back
Some hot bellows under the earth calling my name.

∿

My corpse became your weapon
forced to watch, eyes hung in the air.
The legions you turned to stone.
The girl you pried from her father's arms
using only the threat of my name.

Try to imagine
being so ugly that it petrifies.
To know in the glare of your gaze
what you destroy,
pink sponge of their lungs
sopping marrow of their long bones
transmuted into stone,

your terror, even now as you think of it.
When you see girls at the bazaar,
hieroglyphics made of meat, the trophy
proof of your worth
you think of me. Nights,
instead of blood rolling
into your groin like sobbing
a hollowness in their painted faces
shocks you back.
The fear that i will blossom
in the dark of your daughters' bodies.

Home, curling yourself around your bride
you tell again, how hideous i was.
The things you had to do
to my body to keep her safe,
skeleton key unlocking
her city's bright gate.

And my head, gently
rotting in your leather sack, laughs.

The story you do not tell, Perseus,
do you even remember it?
When you were born—
the fever they thought would kill you.
How the physician found a second heart
asleep beside your heart.

Removed it, cast the bloody scrap
behind your house
raw flesh hatching the snakes
that nearly poisoned you.

And i grew eyes.
In the trash heap. In earshot
of your infant wailing.
i grew legs, the pulpy vise
of my new gums making a noise
that was nearly your name.

Metamorphosis (8th Avenue and 14th Street)

Other times it's so fast you barely know it happened
out the earth-smelling subway mouth onto the sidewalk
it's 93 degrees. i have to walk a block and a half. Behind me

someone's speaking loudly. i look at the sidewalk
telling myself there is no reason to think it's personal
just his inner voice amplified by heat and mad loneliness
i got the biggest dick in the West Village! is not something
he intends to say to me specifically, i think. And then he says *i like*

your legs. My black leggings' cotton weave too thin
specks of flesh tone showing through. It does not matter
the long t-shirt over my crotch or the opaque shorts underneath
doesn't matter the undershirt tight enough, nearly, to bind

doesn't matter that when he says *Biggest dick in the West Village*
Your legs   Wanna ride it   Wanna fuck   that he may
not know what he's offering to put it into. i can't turn around
because then i would rupture the fantasy where i can't hear
across a few feet of air, but rounding the corner

i use the plateglass front of a starbucks as a periscope
and he's just a guy, thickset, sweating, a white t-shirt
with some graphic i can't make out, mesh athletic shorts,
sunglasses, about an arm's length behind me, and me

a praying mantis spraypainted white and wrapped
in a shallow hipster's outfit   a flock of cracking vocal cords
and whimpering wrists   a man   or woman
                or some third animal
who's spent their whole life appearing to ask for this.

Metamorphosis (Uptown 5 Train)

Walking down the subway steps
i see him
      (hard edged, unfriendly)
notice me, a crest
sewn with plastic rhinestones on the back
of his plastic jacket, cheap opulence
betraying itself.

He's Black, black Yankees cap
with the rim blade-straight
over a brown do rag's nylon sheen.
i pretend not to watch, White queer
on my New York Shit

It's 7:45 on a weekday morning
the train's human throng surrounding and obscuring us
the daggers he stares at the side of my white faggot face
      (its nosering, its lipstick)
clearing the path through a plethora
of slithering lives that web
through the trains' incubating bellies.

For 30 blocks the human swarm is packed so close
i think i've lost him then in midtown
it thins out. i sit in the corner of the car
and he's standing above me.

i wonder if he's going to hit me, wonder
who loved him best of all, where she is now
why she can't save him.

i am avoiding his face for fear's sake
but he can't be more than seventeen
the city bursts forth its weaponized young.
i spread a book in my lap
still feigning ignorance of what's between us
      (down the bench, a row of people
      variously preoccupied
      with small devices)

Level with my eyes, his pants sag
below his demons. At first i think
that i'm imagining the way he pivots his hips
into an angle where i'm their only audience.

Then he reaches down for the flesh ellipse
outlined under heather gray cotton
he strokes it turgid into my face.

      (We pass
      like this)
from midtown into Harlem
the metal door between traincars
pressing shut its rubber lips
i don't look up to see
what he wants to see on my face
i don't know if he wants me to be so afraid
      (i am so afraid)

i don't know what of exactly
how many times can my body prove
it's not my own.

My brain who hates me tries to argue
Isn't this what you've been wanting?
      Haven't you been longing, these
            cold months, for desire
                from someone
and who are you after all
          you've done to start
              discriminating now?

Didn't i notice him, after all, before any of this
started to happen. At 125th street, he has to transfer
trains. i'm getting off. The doors unseal
     and suddenly i'm desperate for his eyes.
     i look over my shoulder
     several times
              He isn't going to follow me?
                   Did i do something wrong?

The lurex thread embroidered
back of his jacket
          the crown
     or is it an eagle, a seal. He never glances back.

Minotaur

Before my birth, my mother felt
the swirling tines of bone inside her stomach
my body the evidence of a curse

i'm not ashamed
to have my father's head
sprung phalli of bone

pushed through my crown
i'm ashamed of the rest—
skin like her skin

marshmallow monstrous
tenderness of my un-hided body
ashamed to have a woman's heart

that knows to get someone to love me
i'll have to saw them off. Choose a
name. Leave the labyrinth.

Because i was too inhuman
to take her milk i turned
to blood. She would tell you

i was a monster in the womb
like she didn't feed me
the red salt of her body

until my tongue flushed like an ember.
i have enough magic to see how it ends
how i'm murdered by a boy with a sword

and a ball of string. i know this maze
but if i left, where would i go?
i dream of singing in the opera

        my voice a bell
    the drums stretched with human skin

i am the secret
my mother couldn't keep

you might tell the world
that you love men
but underneath
    you want the beast

Lucifer Suite

Lucifer in the Porno Mag

ripples his abdomen at you,
unfurls the looping crest of his tongue
across the actress more for spectacle
than pleasure   on this page
he's mostly obscured by the girl's
feigned work   on this page so engulfed
it's like he has disappeared   what is he doing
there?   god's lost favorite
in between fluffers,
struggling through the fused hasp
of the woman   tunneling
looking for himself inside her.
          Finding it.

Lucifer's Blue

          drawn shadows
of his cheeks   cyanosis   cyanide
and still alive. His blood doesn't oxygenate.
Explaining the efficacy of crack   my psychiatrist
describes the lung surface   flattened
becoming the size of a football field.
The last night   before Lu left my bed
i breathed him in
          the shrink explains   like
          water. This is how
he rooted me   the scent   diffused
minute particles   how he'll always be in me

Lucifer – Origins

how was the devil born? a question
about god's fertility.
did he make angels by thinking? did he with Lucifer
think wrong? did he birth them in the womanly manner
or was it painless
neuropathy numb limbs clustering out of blank space
or did he reach into his own flesh or whatever
god has instead of flesh and pull it out
did he sculpt it? were they born like shed hair
fingernail clippings, stray bits of god
that god didn't need? or were they out there
even without him the angels
like shoots of rhizome waiting to be unearthed
the way you incubate a virus
in the warm rooms of your own living cells?
Lucifer a dark part of god's body
infected with light
then the dilation. partition.

you author what will destroy your work.
the integrity of your body splits
for your sin to emerge autonomous.

what it must be like for fathers
to know that what they can't restrain
was once of their own making.

Behind the Music: Lucifer

in the interview closes
his eyes to tell his story better
knots his hands together
the small silver voice recorder
pointing at him. *It's a difficult question*
he sees me cross and uncross
my legs. *i don't know how*
to answer that. i mean
i've always had bad habits—what is self-injury anyway?
Rolling his cuffs down over his wrists.
i ask *Does anything else offer you a similar*
relief? i'm working through a script
which he doesn't let me follow much.
He says *With my father*
being the way he is
there was no real alternative
fat tears springing out of his blue blue eyes
smoking on the table between us.

Annunciation

Above the skull's modest
inverted precipice
thin ivory fending off rot
with its humble bioelectricity, above
the marrow spitting out rank pearls of blood
above the trapped carbon, ozone thinned and refurbished, above
all that, their incensed eyes look down, gastric, limning
the salt edges of the wounds we tunnel into
the planet looking for combustion bypass

i'm not saying that they love us, the angels, nor that they
are recognizable, possessed of bodies, horrors
no, at most they catalog our deeds
or rather
their flesh is that repository
nested like feathers
death upon death
they do not re-member
they only Are
the accumulation
admixture of lost parts

Fear not is rhetorical. *Fear not* an admonition
they know impossible to heed.
The fear is you
          your consciousness entire.
The fear is me.

The President Says to Shoot Up Bleach

to clean the inside, very interesting, they're
looking into it he says   i'm thinking, *inside?*
inside the filth-engine we barely contain.
anything dies when it's finally clean

i've counted days
clean time clawing the folding chair under me
in the church basement
i was supposed to die in my filth
before all this

the president says
to put a disinfecting light
inside the body
a disinfecting body
the president who
i don't like to talk about
says drink bleach
and poison control
centers get phone calls

he for some reason says
we should take a kind of quinine
i guess he must make money
off of it   there's no science
once i had malaria (like a genius.
like a tourist. i was in mozambique) so they took
my dying body and hooked it up to a drip
of antique cures the bubbles in the IV line
pearling and terrifying me
quinine made my teeth ache mosquitos sang

into my ear all night
        put light
inside the body
is actually pretty good advice

⫿⫿⫿

my president dies and dies
last year V_____
who the cancer took quick
and D____ who fought
the tumors blooming
in her sex-part where
her father had found her 50 years before
maybe it doesn't matter
if we try to love ourselves

i'm not sure how C_____ killed himself
i know that he was in Chiang Mai
        (like a tourist
like me   american   soulless   trying
to get some light inside the body)
i wonder if it was what he wanted
the way i often wonder
if death is what i want
the estate won't even tell me
how he died.

⫿⫿⫿

the president says drink bleach
in my recovery rooms

a man says *i remember when they'd slide your food*
through a slit under the hospital door because they thought
they could catch Gay Cancer from the fucking air
bleach bleach bleach disinfectant the lungs the light
of the body blots floating leprous
on the surface of the skin spilled and growing

tents go up in the parking lot across
the street, they're medical
but the men going in and out are in
desert camouflage cosplaying for a war
with something you can see.
J__ went to the health food store and said
    Oh i remember this
we're all out of zinc and elderberry and black seed oil
and bitter melon and all this other
shit because someone read a bad news article
that said it would save us   put the light
inside   a key   an angel   silence

in the hospital when my blood was worst i weighed 112 pounds
veins worming across my forehead
i know what i'll look like
when i'm clean   when i'm dead
i know what i'll look like
disinfected
light inside the body
a faggot
a faggot burning

White Power

after Major Jackson

Unblown heads of wishing dandelions
pretending to be made of concrete.
Weatherbleached fiberglass insulation,
where the roof hurricaned off,
naming itself godbeard, firmament.
Wedding dress asphyxiated in storage plastic.
Steals what it can—queer   black—
ornaments itself
novelties on its snowblind expanse.
Your body won't do it. Produces yellow,
actually, bones, cum, pale cream
upon close scrutiny.
Teeth clamped around the cigar's brown ass.
Severed finger dropped into the milk.
Powerpoint slide explaining how
this is an improvement on an existing idea.
What do you think it means.
What is happening.
How a candleflame looks
confronted with daylight.

did you know some "submissive" men
pay dominatrices to crush
small animals to death
in front of them
to call the creature by the man's own
ordinary name

every transgression is
recorded   we rely on you to be
overwhelmed at the prospect
of an archive

my personal
history as an attempted murderee

i was told women could not be
truly evil so look what i did

i am at my best
when chastened almost into
disappearance
at my best
bleeding a little from the acrylics

Oh yes i know
how to tell
when there is danger

there's danger all the time.

Letter to Her Rapist

The velvet groove inside my brain where i lay her down
my mind rolling over her body again and again.
Was it like this for you? Impossible
to stop? Is that why you did it?

It took her months to tell me
First that my attention
made her uncomfortable
Because it felt
like sex was all i wanted
Then later that she thought
of me as a man
and she didn't
want men

Not even if i love her

Not even if my loins
are a poor red-faced animal
hard to train and groom

Not even if i said
she was beautiful

in fact especially not then

Did you get
what you wanted
by taking it? That's
a real question
If you were ever satisfied.

(lies) Lyre

Monsters came and lived inside me. Monsters came from my head and
set up flags and turrets and guns in the physical world. Monsters shouted
their names inside my brain i repeated them, forgive me. i made a song
of it. The names were a spell that set them free. And turned me into one
of them. Like an animal murdered for its ivory, my life split open on the
seam of desire. The fields of bodies on which i visit what you did to me.
You did not do anything. This is the difference. That i have to let you and
let you and let you go and see how the thing in me that cannot want you
to be happy without me is also. You know. A man. Lonely. Violent in that
manner. i can't stop thinking about your mouth like lost money. Punishing
my body. The only instrument i can't lay down. Rubbing the crux of my
legs like an eye.

(Persephone's Husband
Is Not Important and He Says)

She's sitting on the bed
her long legs folded under her—
eyes sliding away from me
as they like to do like i'm a figure in smoke
like there's a river of information
that only she sees. i want to ask her why
but i don't. When the man took her
(the witnesses said *chased, dragged*)
trapped her under the earth
then she did what she did. It's strange
when you think about it
that fruits are seeds and we
eat them. Sugar harps the glistening
tongue. It bothers me
that that is what she took
not the utility of bread but tart
crystalline skin red and transparent inside its covering
of outer rougher skin. And now
she isn't mine. *i was never yours. It isn't*
ownership she says

because since she's come back
she reads my thoughts
and sleeps six inches above the bed
moaning. i know this happened because
she does not believe i love her. Now i ask permission
to kiss her
air hissing past my seedling teeth. i ask her why
she comes back and she puts her hell-hand
her death hand, gilded-immortal
against my cheek. *i come back*
because you need me. You would die
without the rain. Sucks at my tongue

until it bleeds sugar a seed. Her nipple
the crest of her ribs the cells
of my body and the devices in the cells
and the space in between them. Whatever
life is. Electrical.
Animate. Please.
Please give it back.

Letter to Her Rapist

i know you think
it isn't fair i call you that
You have a different memory
　　found the girl and flipped her
　　　　on her back and instead
　　　　　　of woman-parts a scorpion's tail

　　　　　then she started
　　　　before your eyes, stinging herself
　　until the poison inflamed her so badly
you tried to take it out
with your mouth

You think your crimes are mutable
　　i'm here to tell you
　　　　you ruined everything

　　　　　　i have heard this poem before. Men
　　　　parade their lovers' scars into the public square
demand credit for their own bravery.

Somewhere a child kisses
　　a mirror and another child
　　　　shoves a pin through her own face
　　　　　in a photograph
listen
　　　　She's maybe the only person
　　　　　who has ever loved me

　　　　and now i have
this thread of fire left in my brain

that says she could have loved me if
it hadn't happened

      if you hadn't been inside
         holding shut the door.

After the Virus but Before the Riots

evangelicals set up a tent hospital
in Central Park and hate faggots
and we all say *thank you, thank*
you, thanks. Refrigerated trucks pile
overflow corpses inside
an angel's death aria above the threshold
of your hearing driving mad the dogs
fat roaches skirt the cinderblock
more food more food despite
failures of beauty, infrastructure,
empathy, planning, despite human evil
we live until we don't

here on earth a drug company
sends its men in bad suits
to shove their dicks
into a dry hurricane
of government money *gilead gilead*

here on earth dandelions
which are a weed still insist
on their resemblance
to cartoon suns and cheer
for us. the weather
as cryptic as anything
melts the homes of seals
and spreads heat on the back of my neck
like a lover's hand. Everyone
plays at innocence. We send
them back to refugee camps.
The sky is bled out of its light
by the mobile police unit
one stupid floodlight

and the stars are swallowed alive
which of course makes me think
of come and how
i miss it.

here on earth the dead are making
an army. They master restorative justice
and mutual aid. They welcome me.
They are the only ones who do.

After the Virus but Before

you stopped loving me and the riots started four days later

picture of you on red sheets
                    looking away like a ghost

Heaven a tangled glyph in the helicopter blades

⫽⫽

it started like this:
you arrive in plague time
the rain misting   delicate
sky a gray pearl.
what i see is not what happened
brief and silver
the mind records its own faults
          crest of bone in your hip
gleaming like a moon

history has to start somewhere
even if there is always something before it
              i look at your face or rather its pixel simulacra
and think it could begin

the light soft   silver   wet
falling onto my face from everywhere

⫽⫽

it started like this:
i thought it was going to be another whore year
and it was a plague year instead
so we all learned how to sell pictures

suddenly *safer* and less lucrative
trapped inside our houses the body
viewed across a gleaming styx of monitors
a window with skin nailed over it

you found me
inside the thing i was selling
the plague loneliness leaking into
the electrons you siphoned

the water we are made of submerges us
arrives in the eyesockets   lungs
your voice   sliding through my phone
to become water under
my working hand

Eve in the garden naming
      you do not know me   but are willing
to tell me what i am   the signifier becomes
(i'm begging you) the thing itself

⼁⼁⼁

i'd walk alone at night even with curfew
my neighbors gardens come
to life no i never knew you
it was all on the internet.

the signifier becomes (any actor can tell you)
desire emerging on a fictional basis
is still desire crocus forcing itself
to blossom overnight
i am trying to sound intelligent about it
which is a defense

there is a path i've strayed from
(wet in my hand
      a fool alone)
also cut by water
persistent over millennia
running into your mouth

࿇

deprived of light, the human organism
adapts to a 27 hour day and, i assume, goes mad.

i want to know if you could bear it—
the liquid weight   saline   muscle
               follicle   fat tissue
        the way i smell
i want to know if you could bear
the power i insist upon you having.

࿇

once you invent money people will use it
to try to buy love or human life
         inevitable   irredeemable
of course i wish i were a product
you could desire carnally
as though
         on the other side
i could crawl into the dark
behind your eyes
         no longer a problem of "representation"
invisible and known

⑈

when i saw the picture of your come on your stomach
or when you wanted to send me that picture
your wet breath i knew
i'd ruin it by begging you to come here
collapse the real world into the story
            beg you to put the light into my mouth
and seal it up
as though that were enough to make it real

⑈

the symmetry is horrible and literary.
to remember when i was as you are
a beautiful unnerving young adult.

how it felt to have some stranger arrive
            older
full of fascination and petitions

i'm the man now. monster
cloud-limbs breaking off
and growing back new
a glut of eyes peeling themselves from their sockets
and rolling towards
your body laid against the edge
of the camera's ability to capture

desire becomes horror through accumulation

you stopped loving me
the riots began

i only mean it's summer.
i go for long walks late at night
my neighbors all have gardens.
Everything is blooming.
Hyacinths. Irises. Everything is dying too.

they in fact demand that you fight them
fight "the system." they in fact demand
displays of punk fashion, disharmony, longing
steel bars bent to gossamer
shattering to bitcoin fluttering
ornamentally outside their penthouse windows
kinetic infostreams that remind them of the bodies
of women or vice versa

the news congratulates itself on being right about you
docility restored; a resurrection promised
only you won't be there, cast mold of your face with the eyes lit up
exquisite hidden circuitries

skin a received amulet from a clan
of cockbiting wizards who write
definitions of violence purposed to exclude their own acts

for a long time i thought racism was only done
by bad people in private
maybe just one at a time
and even then
they were embarrassed.

meat /// injection

sex as a site of

revision

The prevalence of the condition
is rapidly rising all over the globe
at an alarming rate
The needle goes inside me
and weeps like a father, silent.
a complex psychoemotional
endocrine and metabolic dis-
order

                            uhh
             Abner Louima was
a Haitian man arrested in front
of a nightclub in Brooklyn i think
in the 1990s and then he w—

the central argument appears to be
that the suffering associated with
menstruation is integral to
      womanhood

      the American Plan is
a one-stage procedure
that can be reproduced a competent
neo-urethra to allow for voiding
while standing. there should be
both tactile and erogenous
sensibility. there should be
enough bulk to tolerate the
insertion of a stiffener.
his defense attorney stated the victim's
smile *was a highly provoking*

act . . . would cause anyone
to have an aggressive reaction
the interplay between genetic
and environmental factors results
in heterogeneous progressive ill-
ness with variable degrees of
hopelessness.

Henrietta Lacks
was a mother of five self-
presented to the clinic the most
disturbing trend is the shift in
age of onset, therefore, it is
necessary to identify patients
at the earliest and provide
appropriate lifestyle intervention

Muhlaysia Booker was a Black
trans woman in Texas she was
twenty-two.   In the image of god
he created them   the needle goes
in and there are two types of nerves
god   created man in his own image
types of nerves that convey sensation
the other controls muscular impulse.
the toxin paralyzes only
one variety there was a public

apology paralyzing only one
set of nerves, much like novocaine
numbs but leaves motility possible
this is the opposite. sensation
without movement. Ms. Lacks

presented with the complaint of
vaginal bleeding but there are
some reports that she knew—had
palpated herself—*there is
something wrong with my womb.*

᭼

‹‖›

There should be both tactile
and erogenous sensibility,
they took Mr. Louima to the
hospital from jail claiming
he was found unconscious
the tumor had special qualities
soft   *bright red*   As in the story
of the gorgon her severed head
becoming a tool of the thing
that killed her   god said
unto them be fruitful and
replenish the earth and subdue it

Kendoll waxgleam swallow
-ing me from inside. instead
of a hole, a field begging for
rupture. i don't get surgery
because i don't think it will help.

‹‖›

⁊⁊

diiiiiiiiiiick dick dick diiiiiiiiiiick dick dick dick dick dick diiiiiiiiiiick
i describe the shape (dick) as needlelike,
meaning thin (dick), unpleasant, like an incomplete
(dick) set of fangs. i describe the shape (dick)
as unmemorable and therefore (dick) ideal
or (dick) as thick in a way which is intimidating
(dick) and therefore desirable
i describe it, (dick,) anatomical and brief,
i am technically enthused but nonetheless
am told to adopt a more cheerful tone of voice
dick dick dick dick dick dick diiiiiiiiiiick dick dick dick dick dick dick

⁊⁊

◦⫴◦

Disease mechanisms when
understood can sometimes
indicate a cure. The cells
continued to replicate when
removed from her body
a holy grail for medical researchers
versatile and continuous f—

after something dies every
-one has access to it but it is
no longer relevant for example
popular phrases in African
American Vernacular English.

        the American plan was a
series of laws criminalizing
prostitution uh keeping
the nonprostitute population
        (uhhhhhhh) (what)
        (that phrasing is awkward) i.e. men
safe of course
this criminalizes the condition
of being a woman or woman
-able, penetratateateatetetetcetera
spreading at an alarming rate

Abner Louima was and God
said let them have dominion
over the fish of the sea and
over all the earth, every creeping
thing, although it is most

commonly indicated in female
to male transsexuals there are
other prescriptions
circumstances when
amputation or major trauma
to the penis has occurred.

Muhlaysia Booker was a Black
trans woman in Texas. she was
twenty-two. The alleged prostitutes
were presumed infected by venereal
diseases for which accurate diagnosis
and treatment did not exist, they were
injected with "cures," mercury, arsenic.

Layleen Polanco's death is listed as
sudden unexplained death in epilepsy
no wrongdoing despite recordings
of guards being unable to wake her
the prevalence of the condition

alleged prostitutes were treated
for venereal diseases, medical treatment at the time
consisted of injections.
                   Layleen Polanco's death
in isolation at Riker's Island
was ruled natural, natural
causes no fault, Sudden
Unexplained Death in Epilepsy
no charges, the brain
exploding neural cascades no charges
to be brought, no criminality, the prevalence
of the condition is rising all over the globe
at an alarming rate i don't think
there is a cure for it

᭰

‐ı|ı‐

uh Abner Louima was in
the hospital two months,
dozens of surgeries.
Under the American plan
the medical treatment
for venereal disease
was injection, mercury
arsenic, unproven caustic
agents. Treatment was
compulsory and not
based on any symptom
profile rather everyone
who fit certain identity
criteria and was unmarried
received—

Muhlaysia was
publicly assaulted and
the video went viral,
there was a rally for her.
She spoke at it. A month
later she was dead.

As in
Foucault's observations
that hospitals predate
medicine we have no sense
of what will bring crime
to an end, will bring
violence to an end, so we

have decided to treat
it with   injections
          mercury   arsenic
                    infinite   tumors

much like when i try
to do something that's
not about you, like
fucking someone else,
but it's still about you

⦚⦚⦚

⫼

                                my urine
turning into cornsilk
cotton fibers   a garment
        made of its own burning
turning my face   inside
        out like a sock

the prevalence
of the condition most
commonly indicated in
female-to-male transsexuals
but also occasionally necessary
in instances of castration
when i was young
i let them fuck me and then
afterwards tried to shove
spermicide gel in with my
finger i have never not been
in a nation at war. spermicide
itself causing small tears
in the membranes of the
                        vagina
instances of castration
most often self-perpetuated
in those with severe psychoemotional
disturbance or addiction issues
more rarely there is a perpetrator (uhhhh)
i'm referring to acts
of vengeance.

surgery
        a false promise
                cleansed
by light
        that i can be solved
by being visible.

⼁⼁⼁

·ı|ı·

                              a pleasing
albeit artificial fullness, fine
lines smoothed as the underlying
muscles are paralyzed, there is
no notable loss of expressiveness
when administered by a
professional. the main force
of the disease process is
like a father, weeping, silent
an egg coming out of the tube
ovipositor tunneling into
the host material, a rope of mucous
from which the copulating
bodies suspend

advances in therapeutics
and information technology
combine to give us an improved
understanding of god.

someone found it out about me
from the way i walked
or left it there inside my body
rotting, sucking up the air

              Abner Louima was uh a
Haitian man picked up
outside a Brooklyn nightclub
the police have decided
that my body cannot fight
in their wars either, sand

in the mouth, in the trachea
slashed open by shrapnel
sand in the wound, in the oil,
in the bank account,
sand in the police report
in her nailbeds, sand
in the satellite image,
the encampment, sand
folded inside the body
as it tries to close itself
back up in a fury of refusal
tunnel of muscle, your
gut another universe
black-red, electrified.

in recent decades its status
has changed. previously
it was considered a disorder
of a defined minority,
whereas it now presents
as a major cause of morbidity
and mortality impacting even
some heterosexuals
a body which is a home which is
a rationale for violence
survival in these conditions
a highly provoking act

hermaphroditism in frogs
      in fish   a floating island
of plastic trash   i cannot afford
      to keep my body intact

pleasure's ghosts like larvae
eating a thousand times their weight

        treatment   protocol
police presence
        injections   of mercury   arsenic
one of
        the officers allegedly
allegedly allege all all all all
all of the officers walked
down the hall of the jail
bragging, holding up a broom-
handle smeared with blood
and excrement

╷║╷

        ·||·

     the body is a
memory and belongs to
someone else. the body is a
history
     petals falling open
their insides black as char
burning black
        as my bitch
heart

Muhlaysia Booker was—
          she was an escort—
               i don't see how that's relevant—
          You can't protect people who don't value themselves. God.

          male and female he created them—

and then what happens?

     on the seafloor it spreads
splits, takes on new forms
shoved out of itself, bio-
luminescence, the tumor
kept growing, immortal
sexually assaulted by
his arresting officers
the second time her name
was trending a month
later was when she died
the central argument
appears to be that the
         suffering

associated with menstruation
is integral to womanhood
severe damage to the
colon and bladder,
severe damage to the teeth
legs severed mid-thigh
there should be both
tactile and erogenous
sensibility, minimal
scarring in the donor
area. there should be
enough bulk to tolerate
the insertion of a stiffener.
the result should be
aesthetically acceptable
to the patient. increased
police presence i don't think
it will help, i don't
think there is a cure for it.
the video is impossible
to adequately describe or
forget, the video

⑈

god created man in his own image.
in the image of god he created him
male and female he created them
at an alarming rate injections,

without my body
there is no medicine
no poison either

mercury arsenic my father preoccupied
with the medical risks
only occasionally says things like
What is that growing on your face
a needle goes into me and weeps

i wound myself to create laws on my body
or the laws on my body are wounds

there is something
            wrong with my womb

the central argument appears to be
i am not murdered
            a pleasing albeit artificial weeping
your corpse repurposed as a weapon
            a medical technology
evidence   *a highly provoking act*

sex as a site of

                                            revision

Well, the best thing my heart does

is turn into a pussy. then into a cock. then back
into a heart. except i'm a flunking magician
so i don't have any say over when it does that.
the worst thing my heart does is tell me that there is
something i can do to satisfy it
that there is such a thing as satiety (there isn't)
if i just do a few small things, it will
stop being hungry *Come on baby* and on like that until
i'm trying to pick the shattered glass out of my knee. until
i'm paying a doctor to aspirate some man's genetic material
out of my body's foulest mouth. the best thing
my heart does is wallow salt-snot tears snuffled
back down its valves and the best thing my heart does
is scream, the glassbreaking note prima donna in floor-length silk
pulling the air inside out. the best thing my heart does
is eat you alive until you're bones and silt
in the gray water of his stomach every possible shudder discovered
and the worst thing my heart does is eat
itself and then the hunger grows double inside
his sucked-out mouth and then
he shits out the world.

Uranus

This article is about the planet. For other uses, see C. Bain (disambiguation)

C. Bain's orbit traces the coldest interior
a nebulous implicit power
from the Latin, meaning *ring*, or *circle*

an opening at the opposite end
of the digestive tract from the mouth.
stellar mass collapses on itself
below this point the mucosa of the internal C. Bain becomes skin
this initiates very early in the developmental process
the midgut herniates
throughout the umbilical ring
and develops almost entirely outside the cavity

One hypothesis suggests
C. Bain was hit by a supermassive impactor (Craig)
which caused it to expel most of its primordial heat
left with a depleted core and axial tilt

("Craig" is residual semisolid waste
consequent to food digestion for example:
indigestible matter, such as bones;
food material after nutrients have been extracted;
or ingested matter which would be toxic
if it remained inside C. Bain.)

most other planets have images
located in the intergluteal cleft
The planetary probe encountered C. Bain
which remains the only investigation at a short distance
no other visits are planned

the expulsion of Craig is a persistent crisis for C. Bain
despite such expulsion being its clear evolutionary function

In animals as complex as a common worm
the embryo forms a dent, the blastopore,
which deepens to become the archenteron

in other organisms the original dent becomes C. Bain
while the gut tunnels through to make another opening
which forms the mouth
characterized by its lack of luminosity
circular muscles constrict the event horizon.

C. Bain passes through the pelvic floor
pushing accumulated Craig
against the walls of C. Bain's canal, peristaltic
waves (radially symmetrical
contraction and relaxation) push the Craig down until the
levator ani muscles pull the orifice up over the material
releasing it into space

despite other symbolic and cultural meanings
defecation is inarguably the primary function of C. Bain

the sideways rotation twists C. Bain's magnetic tail into a corkscrew
in most classes of mammal the orifice
and the channels flowing to it are almost completely separate

There are some indications that physical
seasonal changes are happening in C. Bain.
The mechanism of these changes is unclear. Attitudes
towards sexual use of C. Bain vary
and are still illegal in some milieux.

poor visibility attributable to androgen hormones, also a sign of aging
bleaching C. Bain is common especially in the adult film industry

The abundances of
less volatile compounds are poorly known

The C. Bainian rings are composed of extremely dark material
which may have been part of a moon
(or moons) that was shattered (by Craig)
The third-most-abundant component of C. Bain's
atmosphere is Craig which can only originate
from an external source.
only a few particles
survive this flummoxed reply

In culture:
"C. Bain, the Magician" is a movement in the orchestral suite *The Planets*.

Craig was present in varying capacities from 1998 until 2010; one terminated
pregnancy, negligible physical trauma, whether we believe in such constructs as
psychoemotional or financial abuse as a culture appears variable. In any case the
cost has been total, i hope he's happy with it, happy with himself.

Many references to C. Bain in popular culture and news involve humor about one
pronunciation of its name resembling that of the phrase "your anus."

(lies)

there was a bomb. bomb is a cute word. the shape of a cake. the name of a cocktail or sushi roll. there was a bomb, wielded from the sky which seems like the house of god even when it rains fire or maybe especially then. the bomb i don't know despite the fact that we did it. threads of the tapestry running out of my body. ugly medieval lions, their crossed eyes, their heavy manes. aspen are all connected at the root. it only looks like a grove of trees, like separate organisms. sometimes it's sad to have to hate everything because i myself am hateful and am attached to it, a vestigial limb hanging off the belly of the world. the small tan dogs in southern Africa wild and reproducing in any conditions, and the cockroaches, and the octopi, and men men men men men perching forward their guts from their awkward pelvii, running neckties like threads of blood all the way down the front for a slimming effect, poising brassy wax on the head fake hair that pretends to be a fake crown even this, bomb, bomb, don, even you bound like this into me, even you, exploded by something you'll never see, you can't expel the violence, heaving over the golden toilet, empty foam out the mouth, i cannot expel the violence, whispering *piss on me* in a back room, none of it means we're not who we are. bombs shuddering the earth, trains stuck underground, if i saw a child trying to salve a wound with gold i would feel pity.

Exchange Rate

in my fist a coin of air
to buy my health
from the government.
in my coin a fist
of poison that
ruptures the alveoli
of the lungs,
their soft weight
gone sponge and futile
in my cells a glut of oil
that ruptures the alleles
governing skin color, bone
density, resilience
against infection
in my government a wealth
of disease, illness a coin, in
my body, a prophylaxis
the government pays for,
$67 a pill. in my pill a
government, squadron
of cops beating the blood
into order. In my cops
a medicine that reddens
the eyes, traps flame
in the gut. in the gut
an ocean i cannot
catalog, creatures flapping
their saline wings
the flesh erases
itself, orifices become
more prominent,
swallowing swallowing, develop
minds of their own, new

social norms, new forms of
governance. In my social norms
an orifice, a fist
made of air, coin
clattering to the ground
on one side a face, on the
other a building
in my buildings terror
called "security," in my body
a metal detector,
refrigeration trucks
pulled up to the hospital so
corpses can be stacked
inside. An invisible coin
falling through invisible
fingers. profit from
the manufacture of
an unproven drug,
an invisible finger
edges the capsule
down my throat. my body
relies on other bodies
for its safety. to its
detriment. invisibly, clusters
of pins stab the map of black
neighborhoods a glut of oil
in the economy
my government can't unload
an ambulance made of air
on the internet dicks made of
air in an inbox made of air
sprout coins electric
in my open hand, my

tongue a coin i can't
exchange, my government a disease
my cops rupturing
in my fist an economy
how often have i
told you my hand is
empty as though it were not
a weapon for its color its shape
its history a fist
in my cops a fist in my government
in my lungs a fist
in my medicine in my gut
in my health your health
the lungs curled petal-like
around each other
in your fist my fist
the collapse of a regime
a new world
made of air
glimmering through this one
nearly there

Letter to Her Rapist

i'm the Her this time   (don't call me that)
i've been her'd. He found the her in me.   (fuck you)
funny
          to address you as though you're singular.
                              (i reject the premise)
what would justice be?

what i want is for you
              to have to love me.
          her.
the child you hurt.

funny to address you as though you're singular

          echoing. recidivist.
the new ones like you
take me back again
          redempt—uh   revision
see what you did
my face is gone   a flower   a fondant cake melting
                    my face overrun with its sugar for you

          it never works

obedience to desire
does not deliver me

i still think i might have lived if you had loved me
like you said you did.
                    i might have had a body
of my own instead of this
                    sundial in my stomach
always pointing to the sacrificial hour

no one touches me
now. not even when
                    they touch me.

Pornography in Wartime

the signal is garbled to protect me but
will unlock if i pay.
the vomit-yellow carpet

a television channel
between channels
        i'd find it
i was a child
growing eyes behind my eyes

the girls' scrambled tits bright orange
racked with plosive static

how i learned what we were—i saw us
used   the image harvested from our bodies

how i learned how we fought   as though trying
        to take her body like a territory

how i learned that pleasure would be kept
away from me   because
        it was pleasure

it was meant to end but it never ended

        the war

electric   hungering   i open her back up

the laptop   earth in simulacra

the grains of her body twisted
        falling upwards

O, Earth

dead daddy
let me crawl in your big lap

earth is meant to have daughters
not me, not this

i rot as i live
teeth sluffing out of their nerves
        decaying into song

i rot as i live
like you
        my body inherently an excess

Earth. Everyone says you're a woman but i
know better

No woman ever let me live
off her

No woman ever
hurt me
like that

The constellations are fucking
that's what retrograde actually means

i think sex is where
i died before

or where i killed someone

imagine you knew there were no gods
or gods you'd always be at war with

and then she entered
and you were wrong

Future Archaeology

say it ends now

a volcano or meteor and everything suddenly

      humanless   stilled

What would they

      aliens   archeologists   discover

in america

      the video   soundless

boy walking in the street then

the airborne teeth of bullets catch him

fold him double

      lay him

quick on the black

ground. Spun like a top, a toy. Walking away

the blue throbs of light, rising

around him, sharp gasps of rising dust

which are bullets too

             ·ıǁı·

It happens again   again   again

      acquittal   security camera

      a child's hand on a plastic gun

the mugshot where we suspect she was

        already dead

if they came in a silver ship to catalog

      our ghosts

would they know about

      police

Should we prepare a glossary?[1Ω]

---

1 Ω*Apathy*, n. partition cement tempered steel or other material more metaphysical in nature dividing dorsal and lateral nodes of self leaving parts quote unquote "outside." From the Greek "without feeling."

Selfie, n. wishes like doves falling out of the lead sky. The moment they seem to be flying. My neck vertebra stumpy and screaming for the axe.

Whiteness, n. the color consuming an overexposed photograph. erasure. sometimes conceived of as misperception. the insistence on being forgiven for what's unforgivable. under the heart, an acid grave above it, a dog-eared, researched, palely useless guilt. see also *police*.

White liberal queers, n. i'd rather not.

Beneficiaries, n a man with my face disappears through the decimated side of the tower.

Whiteness, n. quote unquote "neutral" or blood cells responsible for immunity which die and fester into pus a sign that there is something the body is attempting to heal. Heroin-constricted pupil. My tongue in the lavender sunset of her mouth. Home razed to the ground.

What do we love, then? Not ourselves

      & not this nation. Eagle legged night

      tearing at our soft body

my white trans hand in her white trans hand

i live with the violences i've chosen

cop cars like stinging ants

      swirl and contain

the lurid welts left where they've been,

erasures, absences. *Was there anything*

else? The researchers say

      fog humming in their future instruments

⫿⫿⫿

Yes.

      purple   raw-edged   silk spilling.

The man on the subway   singing

Mechanical spiders   tickling the surface of mars.

A vocabulary   finally   for what i am

     knowledge that there are others

       films, talk shows,

imperfect personal spacecraft   "representation"

     i can walk down a street and know

if someone hurts me there will be someone i can talk to

who will tell me it's a hate crime

who won't make me apologize

     for being in the way of the fist

the future   i can be   whatever

     kind of faggot i want

You have to exist in order

to be a target for violence.

     i have been given that. Square one.

·||·

the glory of survival

       her small bright face with its gleaming scales

my mouth on her rough incisors,

against the reptile crevice

       where an ear begins to bloom

her skin shed and doubling around me

her black dress   her body

in my mouth as if i understood it

wings spongy with blood   beating the air

trying to hide behind her own crossed wrists.

       Do you feel unsafe

           with men? Am i Men?

Her sharp mouth   the scar above it

an invitation   a door.

ıļı·

there, where i wanted

      to touch her first

the troubled curve orbiting the eye

where i had only a sense something

had gone wrong and not what

how badly. Towards archaeology.

Towards knowledge   a delicate bone

eventually she showed me the photograph

         Her close-cropped hair

         around a corpsethick swelling.

A public bathroom   2 years ago

     left for dead when she stopped screaming

        ambulance   opiate   disinfect

Are the choices death or

     death and evolution?

᎐᎐᎐

Her wish inside me, a lit match

        she threads

her body through the overgrown gate

     of i   and everything

that ever happened there is waiting for her,

     did she grow from this wound

a vine edging through a hostile crevice

heavy with petals

fierce and night-blooming,

snaking through the earth to find me

          ꘎|ǁ|꘎

The question is can the brain hold

its own death   the fact of its ending.

     brain   might mean

the collective deluge

headlines selfies hormonal

adrenal shared traffic rages.

     before i knew her, the times i thought

What would make me happy?

     Oh right. Nothing.

Kill yourself.   if my only argument Against

     is her mouth

then i take her mouth

her sharp hip working where she thrashes

     like something caged

ıǁı

a bomb goes off—no just a firework

decorative   intended to startle you

Refugees tripped and mocked

                    by journalists

        here's my father

walking though the frame

a reek of cigarette smoke

coming off of him

        she holds to me until it's past

my history

        the world's ungrieved blood

                her skeletal system

cathedral   calling

᪶

nerves   axons   strata

subcutaneous   because love

is deconstruction   you know   porno

autopsy   while we did this

      they bombed a restaurant

we bombed a hospital

    my wanting

        pulled itself up from the ground again

coal streaks around her eyes

        i cannot justify it but i can continue

among my burning

    to love her

        to love us

not because i think love will save us

    or because i think love is enough

    i know it's not. i turn to my practice

and pleasure and duty

    my message to our future discoverers that at least i knew

    to love

your own kind is fearful and radical

      no one

    else will do it.

᭡᭡᭡

Some acknowledgments and gratitudes

". . . and her severed head said to Perseus" appeared in the anthology *A Face to Meet the Faces*.

"meat///injection" originated as a performance score for a work shown at Dixon Place's Femme Fest, 2020. Meaningful collaborators in that project were movement director Katie Kay Chelena and performers Summer Minerva and Stephon.

"The President Says Shoot Up Bleach" and "After the Virus but Before the Riots" appeared in the anthology *In Absentia*.

"(Persephone's Husband Is Not Important and He Says)" was selected by Omotara James for *Luna Luna* magazine.

"Letter to Her Rapist" [i know you think . . .] and "Well, the best thing my heart does" appeared in *bedfellows* magazine.

An early version of "Metamorphosis (Uptown 5 Train)" appeared in *Tandem*, vol. II.

An early version of "Pornography in Wartime" appeared in *decomP*.

Thanks to Tobi and Kate and Red Hen profusely for believing in this project and helping me bring it into the world. And thank you Douglas Manuel for your time and care and attention as a reader.

Thank you to Ugly Duckling Presse—Lee, Paige, Serena, Neelufar. Thank you Sasha Warner-Berry, the real MVP. And E. Wray, Jacqualin, April, Sarah Lawson, Ryan Foster Casey, Lamon Manuel, Rosemary, Tatyana, sam sax, Matvei, Daphne Gottlieb. Trisha and Soda and Jonathan Brown, in New Orleans where i finished the first draft of this book in lockdown in 2021.

X., even though you hate feelings and this is all feelings, thank you for helping me.

Thank you to Ralph de la Rosa, my meditation teacher. Thanks to people i have had in generative workshops, when we finally get the language to be a weird denormalized material that can do anything. i said it before, but this book is for Jordan, i love you Jordan.

BIOGRAPHICAL NOTE

C. Bain is a gender liminal writer, performer, and artist. His work focuses on interstices of sex and violence—the queer body subjected to the extraction of knowledge. His plays have been presented at the Tank, the LGBT Center, and Dixon Place in NYC. He has a social work degree from Hunter College and an art MFA from CalArts. His first book, *Debridement*, was a finalist for the Publishing Triangle Awards. He is a 2023–24 Fulbright Scholar in Leipzig, researching the end of the world.

Printed in the USA
CPSIA information can be obtained
at www.ICGtesting.com
JSHW080147290823
47454JS00004B/6

9 781636 281322